DORIS M. JONES

RECOMMENDED

The
Pirates
Who Found Jesus

WORKBOOK PRESS LLC
187 E Warm Springs Rd,
Suite B285, Las Vegas, NV 89119, USA

Website: https://workbookpress.com/
Hotline: 1-888-818-4856
Email: admin@workbookpress.com

Ordering Information:
Quantity sales. Special discounts are available on quantity purchases by corporations, associations, and others. For details, contact the publisher at the address above.

Library of Congress Control Number:
ISBN-13:   978-1-957618-54-8 (Paperback Version)
               978-1-957618-55-5 (Digital Version)

REV. DATE: 02/03/2022

CONTENTS

INTRODUCTION

This story is about two couples who decided to spend the day on their boat relaxing. Before they left home, it was on the news that Pirates were on the high seas. David, Pamela, Thomas and Mildred had no idea that they were going to end up in deep waters. They had planned not go too far out and enjoy the sun and water as usual. Thomas and Mildred Johnson had gotten back from their vacation two days before. David and Pamela Bryant were waiting to hear all the exciting things the Johnson's did while on vacation. The Bryant's owned the boat.

Neither one of them ever expected to encounter the experience of being captured by Pirates. This story has some interesting challenges in it. It will make you see how God works miracles in our lives every day and how He gets us out of life threatening situations in ways we lest expect. There is some humor also. Read on and enjoy!

Chapter 1

The Johnsons' Accept Invitation

Often, David and Pamela Bryant would get on their boat and sail around the area where they lived. Sometimes, they would go out on the ocean and just drift and enjoy the sun. David and Pamela never went too far although the boat had a compass and navigator on it. David felt that if they were to go much farther out, that they should have a more experienced person to navigate the boat.

His dream had always been to own a boat. Now that he has it, he and Pamela would go on it regularly and sometimes they stayed out in the ocean for a couple of days. David would anchor the boat so they would not drift farther into the ocean while they were sleeping. Their best friends were Thomas and Mildred Johnson.

Sometimes they would go with them when they stayed on the boat for a couple of days. Although the weather changes sometimes, it was a beautiful and clear day. Thomas and Mildred had just gotten back home two days ago. They had been on vacation for two weeks.

They were anxious to see their friends again. Mildred was excited to tell Pamela about the shopping that she did while on their trip. Today, they went and checked on their office, which is a medical office. They were planning to call David and Pamela in the morning. They had missed their friends so much. Both couples were anxious to get together again.

"We haven't seen Thomas and Mildred in two weeks. It's time for us to get together. I had wanted to give them a day or two to rest up from their trip before calling them," said Pamela.

David said, "I was thinking maybe we could go on the boat tomorrow. I think that would be good for them to be able to just relax."

"Honey when do you want to leave? Are we leaving tomorrow morning or in the evening?" Pamela asked.

"Yes, I think in the morning would be better. We can go out early and come home before dark," replied David.

Pamela said, "I will call Mildred to see if they have plans for tomorrow. I hope that they have not made any plans."

"Alright honey, I will go to the boat and check the supplies and everything. I want to check our safety gear and inflatable boat. The water and food supply should be good," said David.

"Make sure we have plenty of sun screen lotion," said Pamela, "and plenty of Gatorade."

"Will do," was David's reply. "I will be back in about an hour or so."

In the meantime, the evening news had come on and announced for people to be careful in their boats. The warning was for them not to go too far out in the ocean. There had been an incident of Pirates on the waters and they had robbed two families.

Pamela called to invite Thomas and Mildred to go on the boat with them tomorrow. Pamela was so excited to talk with Mildred that she forgot about the Pirate warning.

When Mildred answered the phone, she said, "Hey girl! I was going to call you in the morning. We missed you guys. We told our friends that we met while on vacation, that you all are great and that we adore you both."

Pamela said, "Girl, I almost didn't recognize your voice! Thanks for the beautiful compliments. The feeling is mutual. "Is everything alright? We wanted to give you all a couple of days to rest up."

"Yes, we are fine. God blessed us to make i t back safely," Mildred said.

"How have you and Thomas been?" Pamela asked, "Did you guys enjoy your vacation? David and I plan to go on the boat in the morning. Since we are just going to be relaxing, I thought you all may want to join us."

"Let me check with Thomas. He went to the store. I am sure he won't mind because we don't have any plans for tomorrow. I will talk with him and call you after he gets back. It's always good to hear from you. Talk to you later," Mildred said.

"Alright and you can tell me about all the wonderful things you did on your vacation. I will wait for your call," Pamela said.

Thomas came in the house as they hung up.

Mildred said, "You just missed Pamela. She and David will be going on the boat in the morning and want us to join them. I can't wait to tell them about our trip. I really missed them."

"That sounds like a great idea. You know we are blessed to have them as friends. I was thanking God this morning for them. All the years that we have been friends, we have never had a bad disagreement," Thomas said. "That is amazing. Well, they are good people and when you try to live right, God will give you good friends."

"You are right, true friends are hard to find. David and Pamela are great company too. I will call and let them know that we will be there early as usual," Mildred said.

Pamela and Mildred always had a lot to talk about because they had the same interest in life. They used to say maybe they were sisters in another life because they had so much in common. One thing they all had in common was their love for God. God had blessed both couple with a good life and financial stability.

They were Christians and tried to live their lives where is showed. They were true servants of God and were always willing to help out where ever they were needed.

Pamela and David thought it was a great day to go on the ocean in their boat. They like to just float and enjoy the sun and the scenery but they were always careful not to drift too far out.

Usually if they felt sleepy, they would anchor the boat so they wouldn't drift while they slept. They both had always lived by water, either the ocean or a big lake. When Thomas and Mildred moved in the neighborhood, they all became good friends.

It's a small community in Hobart, Florida. The weather was always nice and serene. To them it was the perfect place to live. This community was a great place for retired seniors, although some of the people still worked locally. The ages of the people was about sixty and up.

Everyone was very friendly. Maybe that's because they could enjoy life now. Thomas and Mildred arrived early at David and Pamela's home. David went to the door when he heard the doorbell. It was Thomas and Mildred at the door.

David told Pamela, "That must be our friends at the door, I will get it."

Pamela said, "O.K. Honey."

When David opened the door, he said, "Welcome home strangers."

Thomas and Mildred both said, "We are glad to be home."

They all started laughing because they said it at the same time.

Pamela came in and asked, "What is all the laughing about?"

Mildred said, "We are so glad to be home that we said it at the same time. How are you all doing? We really missed you guys."

Pamela said, "I am great. Just glad you all made it back safely.

"We had a great trip," Thomas said, "and we are glad to see you guys."

"Let's head for the dock. We can load the boat. The weather is nice, so I figured we could spend the whole day on the water, if you all don't have other plans." David said. "We really don't have other plans either. We missed you all."

Thomas asked, "Well, what are we waiting for? We can tell you all about our vacation on the boat. Our plans are to spend the day with our best friends. You know, we really missed you guys. I told Mildred this morning that I was thanking God for both of you."

"We have a lot to share with you all," Mildred said. "Anything new happened while we were gone?"

Pamela said, "Nothing special. It was a little quiet but we had a new couple join our group at the Center."

They gathered everything and headed for the boat. Thomas and Mildred had brought some water, snacks, and wine. In the boat, they always kept blankets, life jackets and first aid supplies. After they reached the dock, they were all excited because they loved spending time on the boat. It was only ten minutes from their homes and that was a plus.

After they arrived and put everything away, they

they gathered and prayed. Then they headed out into the water. Usually they go out for 3-4 hours, sometime all day. Today they were planning to stay until evening. Neither couple had anything special to do later, so they were just going to enjoy each other's company.

MIldred said, "Girl, I can't wait to tell you about our trip and show you the things that I bought. I bought you a gift and forgot it on my bed but I am not going to tell you what it is."

Pamela said, "And you mean you would do this to your best friend, huh?"

"I sure will, " Mildred said and smiled. "You are going to love it."

Pamela said, "I had better like it since it's a secret. There is nothing like anticipating a gift from your friend and you don't like it."

Mildred said, "Oh, don't worry about it. You know I have good taste in things."

Pamela said, "Oh alright. I still love you."

"You had better, was Mildred's reply."

David said, "Well we are here let's enjoy the day."

Thomas said, "This is what I have been waiting for. Let's get it on!"

They got out of the car after David parked it and headed for the boat.

Mildred told Pamela, "It is great our guys get along so well."

"Pamela said, "I enjoy all of our friendship together and we love spending time with both of you."

Mildred said, "You know having great friends is next to having a great family."

Pamela said, "That is so true."

Chapter 2

How the Couple Met

David and Pamela Bryant had moved to Hobart, Florida ten years ago. They thought it was such a quiet and peaceful place to retire. They had visited the area with friends and fell in love with the place. When they got back home, they began to make their plans to retire there. This was a happy place for them.

They had family and friends that were left but this was a place that they could afford to live comfortably with their savings and retirement pensions. In Hobart, they had made a lot of friends. Thomas and Mildred Johnson had become their closest friends. They met eight years ago. As a couple, they had so much in common.

David and Thomas used to work programming computers but with different companies. They both loved their work but had retired early. The salaries that they were paid made their retirement possible.

Pamela and Mildred both worked in the medical field before retirement. Mildred was Head Medical Administrator of a Hospital and Pamela was a Registered Nurse.

They found it very interesting how their lives were similar. David and Pamela had three children (two girls, one boy) and Thomas and Mildred had three children (two boys and one girl). Their children were almost the same ages, just months apart or one year apart.

The Johnsons came from New Hope, Alabama and the Bryant's came from Newberg, Mississippi. The Johnsons were African Americans and the Bryant's were Caucasians. Just by faith both families found this little town where everyone loved and got alone with each other.

Sometimes their friends Brian and Marsha Fennegan did things with them. They were an Irish couple and strange enough Brian used to work fixing computers for businesses. Marsha was a Registered Nurse and used to work in the Intensive Care Unit at a hospital.

When they talked after meeting at the Center, Marsha said, "What a small world. It's amazing how we all have so much in common."

She and Brian have two children that are in the same age range of the other children.

"God allows people to come into our lives for a reason and sometimes only for a season," said Pamela.

They are members of the same church. They live a couple of streets from each other in the same neighborhood. Each couple work in different ministries at their church. They all are dedicated in helping people no matter what was needed.

Brian said, "It's so nice to meet people that you can relate to with no problems. We had nice friends back home too."

"When you show yourself friendly, it's easy to attract the right people in your life. We have been truly blessed to have all of you in our lives," David said.

"Having wonderful friends will make retirement more fun. We love you guys and thank God for bringing us together. As long as we are honest with each other, we should never have any problems. We will stand together and if anyone needs help with anything, we will be there for you," Thomas said. "I am sure we all are going to be great friends."

Marsha said, "That's what friends are for; to be there for each other. We are excited that we all have bonded so well and we love all of you."

"Alright now, we don't want tears flowing here. We all love each other and that's good enough for all of us. God is good all the time. Now let's talk about something else," Mildred said.

They all started laughing and hugging each other.

Pamela said, "To a long life and wonderful friendships and maybe one day, we will have a lot of grandchildren among us."

They all laughed because both couples had been waiting for news of a grandbaby.

"That will be awesome!" David said, "I am still waiting for that day."

From that day forward, these three couples were constantly doing things together. They shared birthdays, anniversaries, etc., together. While Thomas and Mildred were on vacation, Brian received a call that his Dad was very ill. Marsha told Brian that she would notify David and Pamela that they would be going out of town. She dialed their phone number as her hand shook. She was very nervous about Brian's Dad because they were very close.

Ring! Ring! Pamela answered the phone with, "Hey there!" She recognized the number and knew that it was either Brian or Marsha.

Marsha said, "Pam, we just got a call that Brian's Dad is very ill and we will be leaving as soon as we pack. I just wanted you guys to know we are leaving so you wouldn't be worried if we didn't answer the phone. We will have our cell phones with us."

"I am so sorry to hear that. We will keep him in our prayers. Let us know when you get there. We will keep check on your home while you are gone. Give Brian our regards," said Pamela.

"Thanks Pam. We appreciate you guys and I will talk with you soon if it's God's will," said Marsha.

"O.K. hon and you all be safe," Pamela said. "Know that we have you all in our prayers too."

Marsha said, "OK and thanks again. Good-bye."

"Bye now," said Pamela. Just as Pamela got off the

phone, David came into the room. When he looked at her, he saw tears rolling down her cheeks.

David asked, "Honey, what's wrong?"

"Brian's Dad is very ill. He is such a nice man. They are getting ready to leave now," replied Pamela.

"Wow! Do they know what's wrong with him?" David asked.

Pamela said, "I don't know. It was such a shock that I didn't think to ask what happened. When we saw him a couple of months ago, he looked good and healthy."

"We know that things can change in our bodies at any moment. We must pray for him and his family," David said.

Pamela said, "Of course, we will pray for him and for safe traveling for Brian and Marsha."

"I am so happy that they don't have a long trip to Brian's Dad," David said. "A one-hour drive is not bad but it may seem longer to them."

"I am going to call Pastor Higgins and ask him to put Brian's Dad on the prayer list," Pamela said.

David replied with, "That's a great idea."

After Pamela got off the phone with their Pastor, David asked, "What time are we going to the Center this evening? Are we going before or after dinner?"

"Well, we can leave after dinner if that's good for you," She answered.

"I think I'll play Bingo tonight. It's been a while since I played," David said.

"That sounds good. It's nice to switch up on the games every now and then. Besides, maybe we will win the big pot for once, "Pamela said.

HaHa!" David laughed.

Pamela's response was, "Yeah, right! We never win big. HaHa!

"Alright now," Davis said. "Tonight, could be the night to win a great prize. You know it is a matter of numbers. The more we play, the better chances of winning big."

Pamela said, "You are right but it seems like it's taking forever."

They laughed as he hugged her and kissed her on the forehead.

Pamela said, "I love you, honey. We have been so blessed."

"I love you too, my dear. You are the best and I always thank God for you," David said.

Bingo is a big past-time thing for elderly people.

A lot of Senior Citizen Centers and Churches have Bingo Games set up so seniors will have some form of recreation.

Chapter 3

Captured By Pirates

Today, they all were excited to be together again and were a little tired. Thomas and Mildred had went below to take a nap. Yesterday was their second day back home from their vacation.

They did a lot of riding from one family's home to the next, trying to visit everyone in two weeks. After three hours, Thomas and Mildred came on deck and David and Pamela were asleep.

"Wake up sleepy heads," Thomas said as he laughed.

"Wow! What time is it?" David asked. I didn't realize I was that tired, although I was up late last night."

Mildred woke up and said, "I guess with no one to talk too, I fell asleep too." They all laughed.

"Well it's snack time. Is anyone hungry?" David asked.

Mildred said, "I will get the snack try."

"I will get the wine glasses and a bottle of wine," Pamela said.

David said, "It is so relaxing on the water. I just love it. I've always dreamed about living like this."

"No cares or worries. It's awesome," said Thomas. "I didn't think that I would live to see this happen."

Thomas and Mildred told them about their vacation and all the family they saw and the things they did. They laughed and talked and were enjoying themselves when David noticed he couldn't see land from any direction. Looking around, all he could see was water.

David said, "I think we have gone too far into the ocean. I always anchor the boat when we get sleepy. I guess sleep came on suddenly."

David got up and Thomas followed him to the Helm. Pamela and Mildred stayed on the deck. David checked the compass and it wasn't working.

Thomas said, "I think I had better call the Coast Guards. We don't want to be here after dark."

"I always check in with them every two hours when we come on the water. I fell asleep. Call them now so they won't be concerned," said David. When Thomas tried to use the radio to call for help, it

was not working either. Thomas looked at David and said, "The radio is not working either! What are we going to do?"

Panic was beginning to take over the both of them. They didn't know where they were or how far they were from their homes. David and Pamela had heard about Pirates being on the high seas but they don't usually go that far out.

On the news it was stated that the Pirates had robbed some people and held them hostage for large sums of money. David and Thomas had seen a lot of Pirate movies in the past and did not want to think about real Pirates. By now, Pamela and Mildred came to see what was taking them so long to come back on deck.

Thomas said, "We have bad news. We are lost!"

Mildred said, "What do you mean? Lost! That's why they have a compass and radio so if one is not working, you can still get help."

"Yes! We have a radio and compass. You mean they

both are not working?" Pamela asked.

David and Thomas answered, "Nope!"

Pamela asked, "What would make them both to not work at the same time?"

"Maybe some type of magnetic force or interference of some kind," Thomas said.

"You don't think we are in the area where the Pirates are, do you?" Pamela asked.

"Honey, we really don't know where we are?" David said.

"What Pirates?" Mildred and Thomas asked.

David said, "Well, it was on the news that some Pirates had taken some people hostage. It stated that they were on the high seas. I wasn't worried because we never go that far in the water."

Pamela asked, "What are we going to do?"

David replied, "The number one thing is prayer and right now, that's the only thing."

It was beginning to get dark. They had left early the morning. Their plans were to spend about six hours out and come in before dark. Before they fell asleep, they were having a good time in conversations, that they did not realize that something was wrong. Mildred and Pamela had been discussing church activities and their children.

After they finished praying, all of a sudden Pamela looked up. She had an expression on her face that scared all of them.

She said, "That boat looks like it's coming toward us!"

David said, "They should know better than that. They are driving too fast."

Just as David finished talking, the boat was there, real close to them. Then they all realized that it wasn't a regular boat. All of a sudden, they heard a voice on a mega phone.

The voice said, "How many are on your boat? If anyone is below, come on the deck. Right now!" That was the voice of Pirate Julio Guerrero. He was a big husky man with a long beard.

Pamela said, "It must be the Coast Guard."

As the boat got closer to them, they could see men dressed in black. Now they realized that it wasn't the Coast Guard.

Mildred said, "Wha..ah..the heck! It's Priates!!

Thomas and David said, "Pirates! Oh my God!

They all stood up shaking in their shoes. Then thunderous voice asked, "Is anyone else aboard?"

It was the voice of Captain Pujet. He was a tall, well-built and handsome man with a beard. Everyone was so nervous that they didn't answer him. You could almost hear their knees knocking. They were just staring at the Pirates and couldn't say anything.

He asked again, "Is there anyone else aboard?" They all said, "Nooo," in trembling voices.

David took Pamela's hand and Thomas hugged Mildred and pulled her close to him.

Captain Pujet asked, "Where y'all headed?"

You see, while they were asleep, the boat wasn't anchored and had drifted too far out. They had drifted three hours out farther than they normally go and they had not noticed it. That was why they all were sleepy. The ocean water has an effect on you, like a hazy day. Pirate Pete told them to climb aboard their ship.

He told them to hurry. They were so afraid that they could barely walk. David and Pamela had heard on the news before they left that there were Pirates on the water. Of course they never expected an encounter with them. Pirates were usually on the high seas. Not today! David thought.

David asked, "What do you want? We don't have any money. We were just relaxing on our boat."

Captain Pujet said, "You are in my territory. Now you and your boat belong to me."

When they got on the Pirate ship, Pirate Pete Hernandez pushed each one of them as they passed him. He shoved them so hard they almost fell.

This angered Thomas very much and he turned to Pirate Pete Hernandez with an angry expression and said, "Keep your hands off my wife!"

"Shut up! Pirate Pete said, "Before I put my hands on you. Y'all are our hostages and you will do what I say."

"Hostages!" Pamela and Mildred said at the same time.

It was about fifteen Pirates. Some of them were

mean and they looked angry. Most of them were good looking men with beards. They could tell that Captain Pujet was the main man.

Pamela and Mildred started praying out loud. They were so nervous, that's all they could do. Praying was the only thing that came to their minds to do. Impulse!

Pirate Pete shouted as he looked at them, "Shut up!"

They kept right on praying like they didn't hear him. They both had their eyes closed. Pirate Pete walked over in front of them and said, "If y'all don't shut up, I will feed both of you to the sharks."

Then Pamela and Mildred opened their eyes and tears were running down their cheeks. They stopped praying out loud. But these two women weren't nearly about to stop praying. They were silently praying.

David said, "Leave them alone. They haven't done anything to you."

Thomas asked, "What do you want with us? We

don't have money or any expensive jewelry. We were minding our own business, relaxing on the boat."

Captain Pujet had come over to them and said, "We may need y'all for negotiations."

"Negotiations? For what?" David asked.

"You will see in due time. Put them below with the others," Captain Pujet ordered.

In the meantime, evening is creeping upon them. No one knows where they went or how long they were to be gone. David and Pamela went on their boat so often that when Thomas and Mildred were with them, they never thought to tell friends or their Pastor where they would be. David would always notify the Coast Guards to let them know that they were on the water.

In a million years, they didn't expect anything like this to happen to them. David would normally check in every two hours. They were guided below in the ship. Pamela and Mildred were taking in all they could see. They looked at every Pirate that they passed. They wanted to remember as much as they could if they got out of this alive.

David and Thomas were trying to see if there was a way that they might be able to escape with their wives.

Also, their roving eyes were looking for weapons that they might be able to get if they were going to try and escape. All four of them were thinking of things that might help them later if they weren't killed.

As soon as they were put in a cabin below in the ship, Pamela and Mildred started praying out loud again. They figured that the Pirates probably would kill them any way so they might as well praise God while they could.

After the ladies finished praying, they started singing. Some of the Pirates thought it sounded good. It broke the boredom and made them homesick. Some of the Pirates started singing with them until Pirate Pete told them to stop.

Of course, when Pamela and Mildred heard the Pirates singing with them, they began to figure maybe they could win them over to help them. After they heard Pirate Pete tell the other Pirates to stop singing, they kind of lost hope but, they weren't going to give up. It was The

Boss (Juan Miguel Ramos) who they needed to win over to let them go but he wasn't on the ship. The Pirates had raided their boat and took everything that they could eat and use. When dinner time came, the couples were brought small portions of food and some of it was from their boat. David and Thomas were more afraid for their wives.

They prayed that they would not be harmed or assaulted in any way. David remembered that he always contacted the Coast Guard before they went out. This was a habit and he had forgotten to call in two hours. He just forgot this time.

It's now going on five hours. By now, the Coast Guard were concerned because they had not heard from David. Coast Guard Sgt. Dayton knew this was not like David to not keep in touch. He was concerned and since they knew about the Pirates, it made him a little nervous although he knew that David and Pamela never went too far out in the water. But he had no way of knowing if the Pirates came in closer.

He said, "We are not getting a response from the Mild Lady. It seems that the radio may not be working." Captain Peters said, "We should send a search crew. Just hope they haven't gone too far and run into those Pirates."

Sgt. Dayton pointed to the map and said, "This is the area were they usually be. They have never gone real

far out before. We will have the crew to check it out and report in as soon as they find out anything. We must remind the crew to be extra careful too."

Captain Peters said, "That sounds like a plan. Just keep me informed."

In the meantime, the two couples were very frightened of the Pirates. They were mean men and they all needed to shave and looked and smelled like they needed to bathe.

Thomas asked, "Where are you taking us?"

Pirate Julio Guerrero said, "Y'all will see when y'all get there. Now I want y'all to sit down and be quiet."

Both couples sat down in the cabin as they were instructed. They were wondering what was going to happen to them and if they would survive this ordeal. They thought about their families and their Pastor.

David looked at Thomas, Mildred and at his wife

Pamela. He was thinking that he and Thomas were in pretty good physical condition at fifty-five years old but not sure if they could handle the Pirates.

Both couples were constantly looking around to see if they had a way to escape and possibly get a weapon. David's main concern was, would they be able to get into a dingy boat safely with their wives and get away. He didn't think that was a good idea.

He told Thomas, "We shouldn't try anything right now. We don't know where we are or how to get home from here. And we don't know if we would be able to get our wives."

"You are right," Thomas responded. "It's too dangerous for all of us."

David's boat was tied to the back of the Pirates' boat. He knew if they could get it loose and get in it, the radio and compass was not working. There were flare guns on his boat but there was no guarantee that the Coast Guard would see them, if they were able to get on their boat. Since it was a dingy boat they would not be able to get away from the Pirates. Besides that, they didn't want to take a chance on their wives getting hurt or killed.

Pamela started singing, Lord Hold My Hand. The other three joined in. They sang in their church choir and were very good. The Pirates liked their singing and was glad to hear them singing. They were on the water most of the time. They didn't have a regular life.

The Pirates were too busy terrorizing people and taking them hostage. Some of them began to feel homesick. Most of them had been away from their families so long that they may not be able to find them. They stopped singing and Mildred started praying.

This was really getting next to some of the Pirates, especially when she asked God to forgive the Pirates for taking them captive. Pirate Pedro Hernandez came over and said, "I think it's time for you all to be quiet."

He sounded almost apologetic. Mildred stopped praying out loud but continued silently. Finally, Pirate Pedro Hernandez came and told them that Capt. Pujet wanted to see the ladies in his cabin. They were nervous because he had told them stop singing and praying and they ignored him, at first.

Captain Pujet said, "Are you ladies always stubborn.

If you don't want any trouble, you will do what you are told. I don't want you stirring my men up out there. Do you all understand?"

"Yes Sir." Mildred and Pamela answered at the same time.

"Alright, now that we understand each other, you can go back to the cabin," Capt. Pujet said, "Julio Guerrera will be giving y'all instructions in about an hour or so."

As they were leaving his cabin, their knees were weak and shaking. The Captain had such a hard and demanding voice. As Pamela and Mildred came up out of the Captain's cabin, David and Thomas was standing by waiting for them. They were silently praying for their wives because they are so much alike.

David and Thomas were afraid that their wives would say something that angered Captain Pujet. Everything had gone well and they were unharmed. When the ladies saw their husbands, they practically fell into their arms.

David and Thomas asked, "Are you alright?" They both spoke at the same time.

Their wives answered, "Yes, we are ok. We were just a little nervous of what was going to happen."

They all were taken back to the cabin they were in. Captain Pujet wanted to make sure the ladies understood the position that they were in. He had told them that he was in control and if they wanted to remain safe, they needed to pay attention to the orders that were given to them. Pamela and Mildred realized that Captain Pujet was serious so they decided that they would be more careful.

Mildred said, "We don't want to push him over the edge. He just may throw us off the ship."

Pamela said, "We can be a little quieter but we will continue to pray so he can't hear us. He can't stop us from praying. We are going to keep on praying until we get released."

Chapter 4

They Met the Boss

After they were put in a room with other people, Pamela begin to cry. She was so scared and frustrated.

David asked, "Honey, don't cry. We are in God's hands.

Pamela said, "I am so angry and scared. Do you think they will let us go?"

"We all are afraid but we are going to be alright," said David.

Thomas said, "We need to pray and let God handle this situation."

"How long do you think they will keep us?" Mildred asked.

Thomas said, "I don't know but looking at these people, it may be a long time. It's best to do what they say."

One of the women said, "Hi, I'm Sandra Brown and this is my husband Brian."

Brian said, "These are some rough characters. Just do what they say and you will be alright. The food hasn't

een too bad. The Captain had the lady prisoners cooking the meals. So far, they have not put hands on any of us."

They each had a thin mattress and one blanket to sleep on the floor. There was an inside bathroom with running water. It was ten people in this room when the two couples were brought in. They made fourteen people.

The next morning Julio Guerrero came and took Thomas and David to Juan Miguel Ramos. He was the one who decided where to put certain captives. Mildred and Pamela were afraid that their husbands were going to be killed.

Sandra Brown said, "They will be taken and questioned." "Then what will they do?" Mildred asked.

Brian Brown said, "They will be brought back here and later, decide if they will put them somewhere else."

Sandra Brown asked, "What kind of work do you all do?"

Pamela said, "We all are retired. Mildred and I worked in the medical field and our husbands were computer technicians."

"You all will probably be taken to live in the Captain's big house. It's a lot better than here," Sandra Brown said.

"Why is that?" Mildred asked.

"Y'all are valuable to them. The Pirates have been getting sick a lot. They need someone to take care of them," Sandra Brown said.

Pamela and Mildred started praying with the other hostages. They prayed for God to intervene and free all of them from the Pirates. About two hours later, Pedro Hernandez came and got Pamela and Mildred.

He said, "Come on you two ladies. I'm taking you to see The Boss, (Juan Miguel Ramos)."

They both were afraid because they didn't know where he was taking them and if he was being truthful. Juan Miguel Ramos stood up when they came into the room. It turned out that Capt. Pujet was only boss on the ship but this man was boss over all of them. In other words, they robbed and brought the goods to The Boss. Pamela and Mildred rushed to their husbands who were in the room. They were so happy to see that they were unharmed.

Juan Miguel Ramos said, "Here is the deal. You and your husbands will stay in my house. No one will be hurt if you do what you are told. Pedro will show you all where you will sleep."

Julio Guerrero brought their bags from their boat. Every time they went out on the boat, they take a few change clothes because the weather changes sometime. Often, they stayed out for a couple of days. If needed, they could take showers on their boat also.

Pedro Hernandez showed them their rooms in the house. The rooms were next to each other and very nice. The couple was so happy that they did not have to stay on the Pirate's ship.

The couple would be responsible for taking care of the Pirates who was sick. In the mean-time the Coast Guard could not find a trace of the couples. The Pirates had taken David's boat off the water and stored it at the Boss' house.

They found out later that there were many more Pirates there. They took turns going out looking for people to rob. They didn't take everyone hostage that they encountered but they did rob them.

Mildred and Pamela decided that they would start working on The Boss. They started praying over him. Their mission was to pray that God would touch this man in a way that he would let all the captives go. They planned to pray so hard that he wouldn't know what hit him.

After all of that singing and praying on the boat, the Pirates were beginning to wander about normal life again. Some of them began to miss their families and wondered what they were doing and if they still lived in the same place.

Pamela and Mildred made their plan. Every morning they would pray and after they pray, they would sing a song. Each morning, the prayer would be the same but the song would be different. They believed by doing this, the songs would eventually get in the head of The Boss.

If they can crack the Boss, it's all over. They know that God answer prayers and with their belief, they knewthey would be freed. They aimed to win him over a little at a time. After they were in the house just two weeks, The Boss found himself waiting to hear Pamela and Mildred singing in the morning.

One day, they asked Pedro Hernandez to ask The Boss if they could speak with him for a few minutes. When they were brought aboard the Pirate ship, it was ten people in the room below and two were women.

The Boss made the mistake of meeting with these two power forces, Pamela and Mildred. They petition him to at least let the two women come in the house so they would be able to take bathes and sleep in a bed.

They said that they would be responsible for the two women and would teach them how to clean wounds and change bandages as well. It didn't take them long to convince The Boss to allowed the two women to come in the house.

After he agreed, Pamela and Mildred went and prayed and thanked God for The Boss allowing the two women to come in the house. Pamela and Mildred not only prayed for their freedom, but for the other hostages as well.

They were always very concerned about the other people. By now they felt like the Boss was warming up to them. They figured, it's just a matter of time and he will be dancing to their tune. These were two smart women. They were not afraid anymore so they got busy working on The Boss. Their goal was to go home in one piece and soon. Now Thomas and David didn't have to worry about their wives.

David told Thomas, "That Boss doesn't know that he is dealing with two strong ladies. Those wives of ours will have him eating out of their hands before it's over."

"You can believe that, especially when they really get to praising God. He will wonder what hit him," Thomas said.

"You know God does things in His own time. I know that we are going to be free. I don't know how long we will be here but I trust my God. He is with us and knows what we are going through," David said.

Thomas said, "We have to give Him thanks. He is due all praise and honor."

Chapter 5

A Pirate Asked About God

The Coast Guard put out a notice on all the channels that the Mild Lady and crew were missing. When the couples Pastor heard this, he summoned the church to pray for David, Pamela, Mildred and Thomas. He also contacted their families so that they were aware of them missing. The Pastor knew the name of the boat.

It's now going on three weeks and no one knows what happened to David, Pamela, Thomas and Mildred. In the meantime, Pamela and Mildred are doing what they are told but they have their early morning schedule of prayer and singing.

Pamela was talking to David and said, "I hope you and Thomas are not still worried about us getting out of here. We are going home soon."

"What do you mean by that?" David asked.

"Well you know that God answers prayers. Mildred and I are working on the Boss. He doesn't know it yet but he is going to let all of us go," Pamela said.

David said, "I've noticed the Pirates are not mean talking to us anymore. And I have heard some of them humming some of the songs that you and Mildred sing. Well, that tells us something."

"That's the key, treat them with kindness and they will automatically respond without realizing it. They just don't know the God we serve," Pamela said.

Mildred heard them talking and said, "Ask and it shall be given to you. Ask not, have not. God is working on them through us."

"They have never met anyone like us," Pamela said. Before they know it, they all are going to have a new attitude because they are no match for our God!"

Mildred said, "I have always prayed for people that I met who said they don't believe in God. I have never tried to convince them. I just pray for them because I know God hears my prayers and He answers them. Sometimes we think He doesn't hear us but He does. He knows when He wants to act on our behalf."

Pamela said, "That's so true because sometime we ask for stuff or things that we don't need. He know what's best for us and that's why He doesn't always answer quickly or at all."

"You know there is always a learning experience in whatever we go through and it brings us closer to God. It makes us rely on Him," David said.

"You are so right about that! Pamela said. "Prayer is the best weapon and it is powerful in numbers. That's how I know all of us are going to be free soon. Hallelluyah!"

It's going on four weeks now that the couples have been missing. They realized that once they relied on God's promises that they didn't need to be afraid because He was with them. As they began to relax and stay in prayer, they realized that the Pirates started talking to them and were nicer.

The Boss started listening to the songs Pamela and Mildred sang each morning. He was beginning to wonder, "How can they sing like that while they are hostages? They don't know if they are ever going home."

He didn't realize that God is now working on him. Ahh, but he doesn't know what they know and who they know. God works in ways that we will never be able to figure out. He knows what He wants to do, when and how. We need to learn to be patient and trust Him.

When we have trials and tribulations, we need to let Him handle them for us.

Capt. Pujet came and talked with David and Thomas. He asked them what motivated their wives to not be afraid of him when he told them to stop praying but they kept on.

David said, "We all are Christians. We believe that God will fight our battles for us. Nothing can happen to us unless He permits it. You see, once you build a relationship with God and read His word daily, you will know that He is your strong tower and He will protect you. It's called Faith."

"How do you get this Faith and this kind of assurance?" Capt. Pujet asked.

Thomas said, "Sir, Faith is the substance of things hoped for, the evidence of things not seen. This is in the King James Version of the Bible, Hebrews 11:1. It's powerful. You must not only read God's word, you must learn to pray to Him and whatever you pray, believe that it will be."

"I know what I do is wrong but I want to start doing things right. Each day can you tell me a little more about this God you all serve," Capt. Pujet said. "Some of the other Pirates know of God but they don't know Him like you all."

David said, "Maybe you can get the ones who are interested so we can start having a short Bible study when you all are off duty."

"I have noticed the Boss listening to your wives singing in the morning. They are very good singers," Capt. Pujet said, "I will talk with the others and see who may be interested."

David said, "I don't know how long or why you all decided to become Pirates but serving God is much better. Believe it or not, you will be much happier too. If you pray with a since heart, God will forgive you for your wrong doing."

"When you are walking with Jesus, it changes you. You will have a new attitude about people and life. The more you read His word, the more you will realize how much He loves us," Thomas said. "He wants all of us to be saved and that was why Christ died on the cross so man could be reconciled with God and be saved."

Capt. Pujet said, "I want what you all have. I want to live a normal life again. Maybe it's not too late for me but I want to be saved."

"Praying the sinner's prayer is the answer. If you confess with your mouth and believe in your heart that Jesus died, was buried and rose on the third day and that He is the Son of God, you will be saved," David said. "Once you accept Jesus, pray and ask God to come into your life."

"He will answer your prayer. His word says, "But seek ye first the Kingdom of God and His righteousness and all these things shall be added unto you (Matthew 6:33)," Thomas said.

Capt. Pujet asked, "What about my bad habits?"

David said, "As you grow in your relationship with God, He will slowly remove them from you. One day you will realize that you no longer have those habits. When you become a Christian, you are not going to be perfect but you will do better. When you error, repent and ask God to forgive you. When you repent, you focus on trying not to make the same errors over and over."

Thomas said, "Capt. Pujet, it's important that you pray with a sincere heart. If you do right by God, He will do better by you. He will bless you in ways that you can't imagine."

"Well I will be looking forwards to the Bible study and thank you all," said Capt. Pujet. "I will let the other guys know about the Bible study also. They will be happy to join us."

"We will be waiting," David said. "This will be a blessing for all of us."

Thomas said, "You all will get a better understanding of God's word and what it means to truly serve Him."

"Yes and one day you will wake up and realize that you are a changed person and some of those old habits are no longer with you," David said.

"As you grow in the word, you will learn to trust God and believe that He will do what He said," Thomas said.

David said, "It's a matter of having faith and trusting. Good night Capt. Pujet,"See you later."

Capt. Pujet said, "Good night guys and thanks for the information."

Thomas said, "You know when we were first captured, I was kind of afraid but as time goes on, I feel relaxed. I guess because I know that Jesus is with us."

"You know, everything happens for a reason. As many times as we have gone out on the boat, this has never happened. God put us here for a reason. These Pirates were beginning to doubt what they were doing and didn't know how to stop," David said.

Thomas said, "He put us here to lead them to Him. He knew that some of them had questions but there was no one on the ship who could give them the right answers. God used us as that vessel."

David and Thomas later got together and prayed asking God to direct them with the right words for their Bible study with the Pirates. After they finished praying, David shouted, "Thank you Jesus. Thank you God."

Thomas and David hugged each other after they finished praying. They now know that they were on a mission for God to save a group of lost Pirates. These guys have been on the water so long that they kind of forgot how people live. Some of them was brought up in church but strayed away once they left home.

Some of them have begun to miss home life. Sometimes we roam in life and don't know where we are going. This happens more with men than women. Once they connect with God and build that relationship, He will direct their path.

David, Thomas, Mildred and Pamela began to pray more for the Pirates. They realized that they had feelings just like everyone else. When people don't have a happy home, they sometimes end up doing things that normally they would not have done.

As time goes on, they heard the Pirates singing some of the songs that Mildred and Pamela sang in the mornings.

David said, "You know that they are not so bad after all. I guess they didn't know what to do with themselves and thought pirating would be fun, as long as they didn't hurt anyone."

"It seems that they didn't really see it as a crime, that way," Thomas said.
Mildred said, "But kidnapping is kidnapping, nomatter how you look at it."

"That's so true," Pamela said, "After all that scares the hex out of a person and some people may never get over it."

David said, "Hopefully they will ask God to forgive them. We can pray for those who were hostages so they may be able to put this behind them."

"It's different with us. Think of those who may not have been saved and were captured. That's a hard pill to swallow," Thomas said.

"We can be thankful that God put us in this situation," Mildred said.

Pamela said, "That's true because God uses us in all kind of ways to reach the unsaved."

-Thomas said, "I will say, Amen to that."

"You know, that's why the word tells us to be prepared because we never know what plan God has for us," David said. "We can pray for the Pirates that God will touch each one of them."

Pamela said, "You know a lot of people have the wrong idea about who God really is and what He does."

"David said, "That happens when parents don't teach their children when they are young. As they get older they will understand it better, if they are taught early."

"That reminds me of the time that I was talking with a man from Germany. He asked me, "How can you believe in something that you don't know about. He said they weren't allowed to read or have Bibles," Mildred said.

Thomas said. "Thank God, we have the freedom here, to read the Bible and worship God."

"Well it's time for us to turn in. You guys sleep well," Pamela said.

Thomas said, "We will see you all in the morning."

Chapter 6

The Day of Freedom

In the meantime, the ladies are working. They are ready to go home and need to step up their game. Their families and friends are grieving over them missing. The Boss noticed how a couple of the Pirates who were ill, recovered real fast since Mildred and Pamela had been praying over them.

Juan Miguel Ramos, The Boss was beginning to have respect for the couples. He was also beginning to wonder about their God. He notice even though they were captives, they were still praising and thanking God. He wondered, "How can they thank God for being in this kind of situation? Several times he has gone over this in his mind. How can they have peace and not be afraid? He thought, "I have never seen anyone like them before."

Throughout the day, The Boss found himself humming some of the songs that Pamela and Mildred sang. The Boss remembered some of those songs from his childhood. His mother used to take him to church. She became very ill when he was nine years old andpassed. They found out that she had pneumonia. His father was so broken by losing his wife, he couldn't deal with it. He took Juan (The Boss) to his sister who was very mean to him. He was an only child. He ran away from home at fifteen years old.

When he was sixteen years old, he met a nineteen year old young man who told him about working on a ship. The young man's name was Skip. He told Juan how much fun they had on the ship. He never knew anything about Pirates. They were kind of like Long Shoremen. Juan (The Boss) joined up with Skip and signed up to work on a ship. He discovered a family on the ship. They all looked out for him and Skip because they were the youngest of them all.

After about three years, Skip decided to go home. This was a sad separation because Skip and Juan Miguel Ramos had become very good friends.

As time went on, Juan was saving his money since he had no one to spend it on. He bought him a boat. At first it was a boat for hire. When he realized the amount of money that he was making and how much he had saved, he bought a ship.

When he was a kid, he used to read about Pirates, and since he turned thirty-five, he wanted to be a Pirate. In his case, he didn't want to kill anyone but he thought it would be fun to capture and rob people. He never intended to hold anyone no more than three months. But since he had captured the Johnsons and the Bryants, he began to have a change of heart.

He didn't realize that God was working on him through Pamela and Mildred. In all actuality, he began to like them. One day he chuckled to himself, "I must be getting weak." Then he smiled. He loved to hear them singing. It reminded him of his Mother.

In the meantime Pamela and Mildred kept reassuring the other captives that they all would be going home soon. They told them not to give up and keep praying. The families were still praying that the couples would be found alive. The church members were committed to pray every day at noon, so they all would be on one accord. The Boss began to wonder how his crew would feel if they stopped Pirating. He was thinking maybe they would stop robbing people because they didn't need money. Instead of taking captives, they could actually help protect them from other Pirates.

The Boss knew that they weren't really bad guys and felt they could turn their lives around. His main concern was would they have to go to jail for what they have done in the past. He figured if they gave back everything that they took, would they be forgiven and allowed to help the Coast Guards do real work.

He was getting older as the rest of the crew and wanted a change in life. The Boss didn't want to break up the family because some of the Pirates did not have any other family. To keep the crew together, he figured if they could work with the Coast Guard that would be the answer. This idea was rolling around in his head.

He figured that they could help the Coast Guard when people were stranded or approached by other Pirates. He felt that they could have a special flag on his ship that way the Coast Guard would know them from other Pirates. Now The Boss (Juan Miguel Ramos) had to figure out how to introduce this idea to his men and the Coast Guard. He thought if they gave back what they have taken and apologize, maybe they would not have to go to jail.

After all, they had never hurt or killed anyone and only had taken a few people captive. He figured the ones who wanted to stay with him could do so.

They could clean up and go off the ship every once in a while and see what's going on in the world. He thought that they could clean the ship up and paint it so it will look nice and not be frightening to people.

His ship had this big ugly picture of a skull head and it was not pleasant to look at. He figured if he changed that picture to something pleasant and painted the ship a nice neutral color, then people would not be afraid when they saw it. He was really serious about no longer being a Pirate. He wondered what type of reaction he might get from his crew. In the meantime, David and Thomas had started having Bible study with most of the Pirates but The Boss didn't know. This shows how God works behind the scene. He will be forty-five years old soon. None of them had died from any of the serious illnesses. A couple of them almost died but survived. He thought, maybe it's time to quit while we are ahead. Thinking about the pain that they had been causing other people, didn't make him feel too good about himself. His conscious was beginning to trouble him. He no longer got enjoyment out of being a Pirate.

It was a very bright and beautiful morning. Pamela and Mildred got up and prayed and started singing as usual.

Pamela said, "Mildred, I think we are going home sooner, than we think."

Mildred responded with, "Why are you saying that?"

"Well, I believe God is about to answer our prayers. I had a vivid dream last night that we all were free," said Pamela. "And The Boss was happy about letting us go."

Mildred said, "It could be the sign that we have been waiting on. We know that God answers prayers and we have been praying."

They started rejoicing and praising God even more so. The Pirates came to see what the fuss was about. They had no idea as to what was happening. David and Thomas came running also and when they saw Pamela and Mildred praising God the way they were, it let them know that something good was going to happen.

The Boss came out and waited until Pamela and Mildred finished praising God. Since his crew was there he said, "I need to meet with my staff in twenty minutes in themeeting hall. This meeting is for the whole crew."

Normally the Boss doesn't meet with the whole crew at one time. There are usually guards at different posts in case someone may want to sneak upon them. But this time, he said, "The whole crew.

David asked, "What happened? I haven't seen Pamela that excited as she praised God in a while."

Thomas said, "I was thinking the same thing when I saw Mildred. But I know one thing, something great is about to happen."

Mildred and Pamela said at the same time, "We are going home real soon. We are going to be free! God is working it out with The Boss. But he doesn't know it yet."

"What! Did The Boss tell you all that he's going to let us go?" David asked.

"No," Mildred said, "but Pamela had a dream that we were freed. We believe that's a sign from God for us to get ready to go home."

"Yes, and since we have been here, when have you all known The Boss to call a meeting with his whole crew at one time?" Pamela asked.
"Well, we know that God has been working on the Pirates who came to our Bible studies. They are ready to do something different and stop Pirating," Thomas said.

In the meeting The Boss (Juan Miguel Ramos) said, "I have something that I want to tell you all. It's been weighing heavy on my heart since we took the Johnsons and Bryants captive. This is a heart fell moment for me and I want to thank each of you for your service and loyalty over the years. We have become one big family but I believe it's time for us to do something different."

The crew started mumbling among themselves, wondering what he was about to say. They were a little nervous because he was different.

The Boss said, "Hold on. I have a plan and I believe you all will like it. I plan to talk with the Coast Guard about Amnesty for us. We have been out here quite a while. Any or all of you can stay but I figured that we will do things differently. Instead, we will assist the Coast Guard in helping people who get stranded or lost or attacked by other Pirates. And we will stop taking captives. We are going to give everyone that we have now, their freedom. I need a vote on this."

The crew was so excited that it shocked The Boss. Some was jumping up and down. All of a sudden everyone got quiet. Then Private Donald said, "What are we going to do? Some of us don't have family outside of this family?"

The Boss said, "Everyone can stay on the ship as usual but I thought every once in a while, we all could go ashore together and see what's going on in the real world. We will always be family and maybe we can go to church together and some of you just might get married."

They all laughed real loud. The crew was really excited now because they all had gotten a taste of

Jesus and they want to know more. The Boss was surprised that he got such a positive reaction when he mentioned going to church and it made him happy.

Now he had to contact the Coast Guard and see if his plan with them would work. At any rate, he is ready to let the captives have their freedom. It's now evening and Capt. Pujet has been given permission to tell the captives that they are going to be freed. The Boss knew that when Mildred and Pamela got the news, he would hear them praising God. As he thought about this, a big smile came on his face.

He was glad that he was going to make them happy. He went into his home office and contacted the Coast Guard. He explained in detailed how he and his crew have found Jesus. He told Capt. Peters that he was hoping they could get Amnesty and start working with the Coast Guard on the water.

He told Capt. Peters that they would return the money and jewelry because for some strange reason, he kept record of the people who they took things from. The Capt. Peters told him that he would have to talk with his Superior Officer and would get back with him in the morning.

He felt confident that they would grant them Amnesty if they returned all the stolen goods and money. He thought maybe they could visit the Bryants and Johnsons church sometime. It will be a shocker for them to see us at their church. The next morning when Pamela and Mildred prayed and started singing, all the Pirates came where they were, including The Boss.

He had told the Pirates to come because he wanted them there when he would tell the hostages that they would be going home. All the other hostages were brought there also. Each one of them was a little nervous because they had no idea of what was going on.

After they got through with their praise and worship, Capt. Pujet, announced that The Boss would be releasing all the captives. He told them that they would be able to call their families to let them know that they were going home. The captives started screaming and crying and praising God. Some of the Pirates had tears in their eyes.

They all were very happy at The Boss' decision. Pamela and David, Mildred and Thomas hugged each other, and then everyone started hugging each other, including The Boss.

They all thanked him for his kindness. He let them know that the Coast Guard was going to let them work with them. They all would be exonerated because they were returning everything they took.

The Boss contacted the Coast Guard to let them know that he was setting the captives free. He called David and Thomas into his office. When they came in, he told them to sit down. The Boss said, "I want you all to call your Pastor and let him know that you are coming home. It will be dark soon, so tell him that you all will be leaving early in the morning. My men will take you close to your home and give your boat back to you. I must say that I can't apologize enough for the grief that I have caused. Please forgive me."

David and Thomas couldn't believe what they were hearing, The Boss apologized.

David said, "Sir we thank you and appreciate you for not hurting us or our wives."

"Just call me Juan," said Juan Miguel Ramos.

Thomas said, "I am glad that we met you guys. You all are ok in my book and I thank God for bringing us to you all."

Juan Miguel Ramos said, "No, we thank you all and God for being who you are and for helping us to see the light. We were living in a dark world and didn't realize it."

David said, "We have to give God all the glory because He orchestrated this. We all have been blessed by this experience."

Thomas and Juan Miguel Ramos both said, "Amen."

CHAPTER 7

The Pirates Came to Church

The Boss (Juan Miguel Ramos) let the hostages call their families to let them know that they were going home. David called Pastor Higgins, their pastor to let them know that they were safe and on their way home. Their church family was already having a vigil for them.

They had been gathering three times a week and praying for their safe return. When Pastor Higgins told the members, they started shouting, crying and praising God. The Bryant and Johnson families were there and they were crying and jumping for joy.

David, Pamela, Thomas and Mildred arrived early the next morning. All the church members were there to meet them at the dock and a news crew also. When the two couples got off the boat, they were rushed by their families with hugs and kisses.

The news reporters were taking pictures and filming them. They asked if they could interview the couple but they asked if they could do it at another time.

Thomas said, "We just want to be with our families right now, please."

David said, "Give us a phone number and we will call you in a day or two. We have had an experience and want to be with our families now. We thank you for coming."

Pamela and Mildred were so glad to see their children. They were all crying and praising God. They thanked Him for keeping them safe and bringing them back. Brian and Marsha Fennegan were back and they were there too. Brian said his Dad was much better and back home. He thanked them for their prayers.

Marsha said, "We were very concerned for you all. We were asking God to please keep you safe."

Pamela said, "Girl we had a scare. We had no idea if we were going to make it back or not."

"It was a frightening experience but God is good. He protected us from all hurt, harm and danger," Mildred said.

David said, "Pamela and Mildred kept singing and praying all the while we were captive and here we are. We serve an awesome God."

"You bet we do. It pays to put God first in everything you do and stay in His word. It was scary at first but we had to keep our faith," Thomas said.

All the people separated and went to their homes. This would be something that the whole town would never forget. The Johnsons and Bryants' children decided that they would stay for that day with the couples.

On the next Sunday morning, everyone was gathering at church. Pamela and Mildred were the praise team leaders. They were getting in position to start praise and worship. Then the church door opened wide and all those men were standing in the doorway.

When the sunlight came in, everyone had turned around to see what was happening. It kind of scared the congregation. They were wondering, "What is going on?" They didn't recognize these men. What do they want? Who are they? All the men were nicely dressed, shaved and looked good.

As they came toward the front of the church, Mildred and Pamela began to recognize some of them. Then they started shouting and praising God. It was The Boss and his crew. They came all the way to the front and faced the members.

The Boss (Juan Miguel Ramos), said, "We are the Pirates who had the Bryants and Johnsons captive. We felt that we needed to come before all of you and apologize for our behavior. I am speaking for all of us. We are very sorry for what we put you all through. Even though what we did was wrong, a lot of good has come out of it. We found Jesus! Anytime that we are in this area we would like to worship with you all."

Everyone started praising God more and some were crying. Pamela and Mildred came from the pulpit and started hugging the Pirates and David and Thomas joined them along with the rest of the members.

David gave Juan Miguel Ramos their address and told him that they would be welcomed at their home anytime. There was hardly a dry eye in the church. This was a glorious day for all of them.

Pamela and Mildred started singing and some of the crew went in the pulpit and sang with them. They were very good singers too.

Juan Miguel Ramos said, "There is one more thing. You see, God sent them to save us. We were on the wrong path and with Mildred and Pamela singing and praying all the time, it opened our eyes. We thank God for sending them to us."

After church was over, all the members gathered around the Pirates and started hugging and thanking them for not harming the two couples. This was an exciting day at their church. They were so thankful that God had brought the couples back safely. They all knew that this was the work of God.

David asked Juan, "Do you all have any special plans when you leave here?"

Juan Miguel Ramos said, "No we don't."

"Well you all can come home with me and Pamela. We can fire up the grill and have a bar-b-que," David said

"Wow! The other Pirates shouted. That would be great."

Juan Miguel Ramos said, "We will be honored to join you all and thank you for being so kind."

Thomas said, "We thank you all for not being real, "Pirates."

They all laughed. They went home with David and Pamela. Thomas and Mildred came also and a few of their church friends. David and Pamela had a big backyard with a swimming pool. This would give the Pirates a taste of how people live.

David and Pamela always kept a lot of food because they never knew when their children would bring friends with them when they visited.

Pirate Pete said, "This reminds me when I was growing up. Our families would get together and cook, eat and be happy."

"Yes, this does remind me of home also. Most of my relatives died years ago. After mom and dad were killed in an auto accident, that's when I left home. Being an only child, there was no reason to stay," Capt. Pujet said.

Juan Miguel Ramos said, "Alright, let's change the subject before a lot of tears start flowing."

They laughed and Pirate Donald said, "Where are the dominoes?"

Thomas said, "Now that's my kind of talk." Pamela, Rose, Alice and Mildred had gone into the kitchen to make potato salad, macaroni and cheese and bake cakes. They had plenty of sodas and juices. They were so happy that things turned out the way they did. But the best part was the Pirates finding Jesus.

Britney and Joshua, the children of David and Pamela came and told everyone that they were leaving. They lived about an hour away.

Britney said, "Now that we know that our love ones are in good hands, we don't have to worry anymore."

"We want to thank you guys for not hurting our parents or the Bryants. We wish you all well and will be looking forwards to seeing you all again," Joshua said.

David and Pamela were very proud of their children because they grew up to be great and respectful people. Thomas and Mildred had said good-bye to their children at the church. They had jobs to go back too. Since their parents were in good hands, they knew that their worry was over.

When the food was ready, everyone gathered and David prayed. After he blessed the food, he thanked God for turning a bad situation into a good one. The Pirates were their captors and now they are friends. Some of the Pirates ended up teary eyed. They couldn't believe that this was happening to them.

Juan Miguel Ramos made a little speech. He said, "I realize what we have been missing by isolating ourselves from everyone. This is very special to all of us. We are like a family and now you all have incorporated us into your families. We are deeply grateful and honored. And I give God the glory."

Mildred and Pamela said, "Hallelujah," at the same time.

They were touched by his speech and were wiping tears from their eyes.

David said, "Alright now. That's enough speeches for today. Let's eat. Everything looks real good."

They sat down and you could hear the chewing and

smacking. The food was great. They were not used to home cooked meals. They had some good cooks among them but this was nothing like the touch of a woman's cooking.

Capt. Pujet said, "You ladies put y'alls all feet in this. It's the best that I have had in a long time."

The rest of the Pirates said, "Amen."

They all laughed. When they finished eating, Pamela asked, "Who is ready for dessert?"

The Pirates all looked at each and laughed because they were so full.

Pirate Donald said, "I think we are going to have dessert later. The food was good and we have stuffed ourselves."

"Ladies you sing, pray and are good cooks," Juan Miguel Ramos said."

The Pirates thanked them for their hospitality and of course they all were happy with the food.

David said, "We have two sets of dominoes. Let's get it on."

Pirate Pete said, "That's what I want to hear."

Rose and Alice from the church helped Pamela and Mildred clean up and put the left-over food away. Both of them were single. They had their eyes on two handsome Pirates.

Mildred teased Rose and asked, "Who caught your eye?"

Rose said, "What do you mean?" She started smiling.

Mildred said, "Which Pirate caught your eye?

Rose said, "They all are really good looking."

Pamela said, "But you can't have but one."

They all started laughing.

"Well the Leader looks interesting," Alice said.

"That is Juan Miguel Ramos and he has never been married," Mildred said.

Pamela said, "OK Ms. Rose, which one do you have eyes for?" "My eyes caught Pirate Pete," She said. Mildred said, "Just be careful and be in prayer about these young men. They have been away from civilization as we know it for quite some time."

Pamela said, "If you trust God and stay in prayer you will know who is for you. Never be in a hurry because that's where most people make a mistake. When you wait on God, you won't have to worry if he is right or not."

"That is so true. When I met Thomas, I wasn't interested in him as far as dating. We became friends and after a while, I noticed my feeling changing toward him. Then I began to pray and asked God for discernment," Mildred said.

Alice asked, "When did you know that he was the right guy?"

"I knew when he told me that he had fallen in love with me. We had just been buddy friends for about two years and he had never said anything about how he felt about me. So we both agreed to pray and ask God for guidance," Mildred said.

Pamela said, "When you truly trust God, you will know when you get an answer. He has a way of showing you things right before your eyes that you don't see." Rose said, "That is deep. I never thought about praying for a husband but it makes a lot of sense. I am thankful for this discussion."

"Sometimes young women feel that they arenot ever going to get married because all of their friends are married. In cases like those, they have to be careful so they don't end up marrying just anybody," Pamela said. "When you start dating, take it slow. There is no rush."

Mildred said, "You want to make sure that you both are equally yoked. You want a man who knows and loves God. One who will love and treat you right."

Rode said, "I am glad that I came over here. This was what I needed to hear and I thank both of you. I have never had anyone to talk to me like this. After Mom died when I was fourteen, there was only my dad and brother."

Alice said, "I still live with my mom but she never talked to me like this. In fact, since she is divorced, she doesn't have too much to say about men except for me to be careful and don't get pregnant. I told her that I wasn't having sex with anyone and she just said, "Yeah." But I guess it's because I am thirty-three and she just assumes that I have been with a man."

"Well, I am thirty years old and have never been with a man. I don't want to be someone's sleep around woman because they won't have respect for you," Rose said.

Pamela said, "There are a lot of single women who are still virgins but they seem to feel it's a shame for anyone to know that. It's actually something to be proud of because God wants us to remain virgins until we marry."

"Don't ever let anyone make you feel ashamed because you are a virgin. That is something that the man you marry will appreciate. Believe it or not, there are a lot of virgin men but they won't tell anyone. Because they are men, other men make them think that they should have sex before marrying," Mildred said.

Rose said, "I guess we both were meant to get this lesson. I truly thank both of you for taking time to share this with us."

"If later I have questions about this type of stuff, is it ok to call you guys?" Alice asked.

Pamela said, "That is not problem. The older women should be teaching the younger women stuff like this."

"Well, the men should be ready for dessert by now. We can slice some cake and dish up some ice cream. I don't think anyone will refuse," Mildred said

They got the dessert ready and took it outside to the men. Of course the Pirates had noticed Alice and Rose. They both were beautiful young women. Juan Miguel Ramos had really noticed Alice. He had started wondering if she was married or had a boyfriend. Then he thought she probably wouldn't be interested in him. It was something special about her. He's hoping that no one else has eyes for her.

In the meantime, Pirate Pete has his eyes on Rose. They have been on the ship so long and now they are wondering how they would approach a woman. The ladies finished serving the men and went back into the house.

Alice said, "I think I should be heading home before dark. I don't want my dad to be worried."

"Wait and we can go together," Rose said, "Thanks again for the wonderful talk ladies."

They had walked from the church which was about four blocks away. They lived on the same street only three houses apart. Alice moved there with her mom and dad three years ago. Her mom passed a year later. Rose was her mom's Caregiver. They moved here about three months after Alice and they became close friends.

In the meantime, Juan Miguel Ramos couldn't keep his mind off of Alice. He was drawn to her. Well this was a two way street because Alice kept thinking about him. This was the first time that they met and she wondered about love at first sight. She wondered does that ever really happen to anyone!

When the Pirates were getting ready to leave David and Pamela's home, they kept thanking them for being so generous to them. Finally they left. Their boat was docked only ten minutes away so they had walked to the church.

As they headed back to the boat, they chatted about a great time that they had and that the people were awesome.

Juan Miguel Ramos asked, "How would you all like going to church on a regular basis?"

They all shouted, "Great."

Juan Miguel Ramos said, "I was thinking that the town close to here might have some real estate for sale. We could start buying a business and some rental properties. If we get a complex for a starter, we all can live in it."

Capt. Pujet said, "That sounds like a great idea. We can get civilized again and it's great that we have found a community of friends."

Donald said, "We can start living like regular people and get caught up on some of this new technology and stuff."

"We can go fishing on the weekends and live normal again. Maybe I'll meet a nice lady and get married," Pirate Pete said.

"Well there are a lot of ladies at the church, some of them are probably single," Juan Miguel

Ramos said. "Maybe we will all get married and I am sure there are women in the next town also."

"Guys we have found Jesus and we want to treat the ladies right that we meet. We want to respect them," Capt. Pujet said.

"Yes we have to remember that we all had a mother and some of you had sisters. Treat the women the way you would want them treated. If you keep this in mind, you will be fine," Juan Miguel Ramos said, "Tomorrow we will make a plan and go to the next town and check it out."

"That will be cool. It's only about ten or fifteen minutes from here," Pirate Pete said, "We will be able to go to church on Sundays and to Bible study on Tuesdays. We can invite David and Thomas to go fishing with us."

The following Sunday, the Pirates came to church. They made another grand entrance. Everyone was happy to see them. They not only wanted to come to church, they wanted to get involved.

Juan Miguel Ramos spoke with Pastor Higgins and asked if they all could meet with him the following week. He told him that they were serious about serving God and he wanted counseling for all of them. Of course Pastor Higgins agreed to meet with them the following Saturday afternoon at the church. As the week went by David and Pamela discussed how proud they were of the Pirates.

"You know it's amazing how God work things in our lives," David said.

Pamela said, "You mean turning a bad situation into greatness. He has all kind of ways to use people to bring other people to Him."

"Wow! When we were captured we had no way of knowing that things would turn for the best," David said.

"The Pirates turned out to be a great bunch of guys. I guess that is the way things go when you have people to rally behind you," Pamela said. "It brings the good out of them."

David said, "I don't believe that most people realize how important family is. If you don't have anyone to show love and compassion to you, I guess anyone can go astray."

Pamela said, "I just thank God that we fell into their hands and not real Pirates. God had His reason for us to experience that situation. It wasn't only for them but it was for us as well."

"Honey, you know you are right. We have learned a lot from this experience. I know without a doubt that we can trust God. We learned that people are not always as they seem," David said. "God used us to plant the seed in the Pirates.

Now they all had accepted Him into their lives, they are happier," Pamela said.

David said, "I am happy for them. Now we have a whole new group of friends. Giving God the glory, I am happy and thankful. You know the Pirates fitted right in with the congregation and everyone was comfortable with each other."

Pamela said, "I have a feeling before it's over, there are going to be a few weddings around here."

"Weddings!" David said.

"Yes weddings. Just stop and think about all the single women in our church. Now look at how many Pirates there are and they all have accepted Christ," Pamela said.

David said, "Hmm! That is something to think about. It was no coincident of us being captured and that's for sure."

"Juan Miguel Ramos told me that they are going to check the next town and look into buying real estate. He said they like the area and feel like they have found family with us." David said.

Pamela said, "That would be great. They would be able to come to church regularly.

"Yes and Thomas and I would be able to go fishing with them some weekends too," David said.

"Well God has His way of working things out and connecting people with other people. We should always help each other," Pamela said.

"You know when I was growing up people were more considerate of other people than they are today," David said.

At Thomas and Mildred's home they were talking about the Pirates also. They were very happy that they accepted Christ and wanted to worship with them.

"We never know who God is going to put in our path. Some are for a lifetime and some are just for a short while," Mildred said.

"We can all learn from each other and learn to share the kind of love Jesus talks about. We need to be careful how we treat each other also," Thomas said.

Mildred said, "That is so true because the ones that we treat wrong may be the ones that we will need to help us sone day."

Thomas said, "God made us interdependent on each other. We can't make it in life alone."

"We are actually one big family. God's family and that's why we should love one another. No one is perfect and we don't have the right to try and judge another person either," Mildred said.

Thomas said, "I am glad for that experience. It was a lesson for us. It showed us that people are not always what they seem to be."

"I am glad too. They are a nice group of men who kind of lost their way in life. Now that they have found Jesus, they are back on the right track," Mildred said. "They really enjoyed the fellowship at David and Pamela's house."

Thomas said, "Yes they did enjoy themselves. They were very relaxed and knew that they were in good company."

CHAPTER 8

The Pirates Moved to Next Town

Juan Miguel Ramos met with his crew and they visited the next town which was Hillsboro, Florida. It was only fifteen minutes away from Hobart, where the Johnsons and Bryants' lived. They bought a twelve unit apartment building. The units were two bedrooms each. This was perfect for them because two could share an apartment and there were a couple left to rent out.

Juan Miguel Ramos had an apartment by himself. The complex needed a little fixing up so they started working on it the first weekend after they closed escrow. There was no major work needed, only cosmetic. They all pooled their money together so after they closed escrow on the apartment complex, they put a couple of businesses in escrow.

The businesses would give them permanent income and they would have something to do to occupy their time during the week. They all were excited about this and the fact that they were still close to Hobart. By the end of the second week, they were moving in.

They missed going to church on Sunday because they wanted to surprise the Johnsons and Bryants of their move.

Juan Miguel Ramos had a meeting with his crew and told them, "Now that we have a place to put our feet down, we can live normal lives again. We will have jobs in the businesses and we will check into that other apartment complexes for sale so if anyone of you get married, you will be able to have your own place."

"That's a great idea and in the meantime, we can rent them out and be earning income," Pirate Pete said.

Capt. Pujet said, "This is going to be fun and we will be able to go to church on Sundays in Hobart."

Pirate Donald said, "David, Pamela, Thomas and Mildred are going to be very surprised and proud of us."

"After we get settled in, I think we all need to enroll in a computer class so we can learn the full benefits of operating a computer. We have to be prepared when we start working in our businesses," Juan Miguel Ramos said.

Pirate Pete asked, "Are we going to take over the workers positions in the businesses?"

"Oh no! I believe it will be room for us to join these businesses, even if it's just part-time. We will have to decide who will be the overseer of the money coming in. I know each of you have some talents that will be helpful so we will have success with these businesses and rentals," Juan Miguel Ramos said.

Capt. Pujet said, "I will get some applications and each one of us will fill out one. This way we will know the best position for each of us."

Pirate Pete said, "That is a great idea and if any of us need to brush up on our skills, we can go to night school."

The rest of the Pirates yell, "Night school!"

"Yes, night school," Pirate Pete said. "Don't you want to be confident in your job? Beside if you get married, don't you want your wife to know that you are a smart Pirate?"

They all laughed at this and agreed. Now they were beginning to realize that they have been out of circulation and need to know how to function in society again. Now that they are moving close to Hobart, they will not only be able to go to church but they will be able to go to Bible study also. They were really excited about this and wanted to know how to get a closer relationship with God.

When they had met with Pastor Higgins, they got a lot of their questions answered but they were still hungry for the word. After they moved in the apartment complex and the following Sunday, they realized that they did not have Bibles.

After church, Juan Miguel Ramos pulled David aside and asked, "Will you show me what Bible that we should use. I want to get one for each one of us so we can start reading on a daily basis. And I need you to tell me where we should start reading."

David said, "I will be more than happy to take you to the Bible Bookstore tomorrow if that's good for you."

"That will be great because we will have our Bibles when we come to Bible study," Juan Miguel Ramos said.

"I can give you the verses that we will be going over this week in Bible study. You all can read them and if you have questions, you will be able to get answers," David said.

"It will be highly appreciated and I thank you for taking the time with me," Juan Miguel Ramos said. "By the way, we were going to surprise you all but I guess this is a good time to tell you."

David said, "Is anything wrong?"

"No everything is great. We bought an apartment complex in Hillsboro and we are moved in. We will be able to come to church and Bible study. We decided that we need to set roots and join society again," Juan Miguel Ramos said.

David gave him a big hug and said, "I am so happy for you guys. Thank you Jesus!"

"All the guys are excited and we are looking forward to fellowshipping with you all. You guys have probably saved our lives," Juan Miguel Ramos said. "Most of all we are very thankful for you all sharing your knowledge of Jesus."

David said, "Juan, you have God to thank for that. He just used us as vessels to reach you all He pulled you in. All we did was plant the seed and God did the watering."

Juan Miguel Ramos said, "Well I have held you up long enough. What's a good time for me to meet you tomorrow?"

"How about 10:00 a.m. Just come to my house and I will drive to the Bible store," David said. "See you tomorrow."

Juan Miguel Ramos said, "Ok, I will see you at 10:00 a.m. and thanks again."

Just as David was going back in the church to see if Pamela was ready to leave, she was on her way out.

Pamela said, "Honey I am sorry to keep you waiting but me and Mildred had some last minutes things we had to do. We are going to start a mentoring group where the older women start teaching the young women about life and trusting God about who they marry. "

"It's no problem. I know you guys get busy sometime. That sounds like a wonderful idea. I was outside talking to Juan. You won't believe it but they have bought an apartment complex in Hillsboro and have moved in," David said.
"Are you kidding me?" Pamela asked.

"He said they want to join society again and put down some roots. They are excited that they will be able to come to church and Bible study. In fact, I will be taking him tomorrow to buy Bibles for all of them," David said.

Pamela said, "Thank you Jesus. Thank you Lord. God you are so good."

"Yes He is!" David said, "Let's get home, I am a little hungry. My stomach is telling me that it's lunch time."

Pamela said, "I think mine is telling me the same thing."

They started laughing. They are happy that God used them as vessels to bring the Pirates to Christ. What they thought was bad, God turned it into good. When David and Pamela got home and settled down, Pamela called Mildred. She was so excited about the Pirates moving to Hillsboro.

Ring! Ring! Mildred's phone was ringing. Mildred picked up and said, "Hello."

Pamela said, "The Pirates have moved to Hillsboro. David said they bought an apartment complex and moved in this past week."

"Praise God, Mildred said. "Wow!"

"They are planning to come to our church each Sunday and to Bible study," Pamela said.

Mildred said, "God is awesome. What a blessing. It shows what prayer can do when you believe."

Thomas came into the room. He wondered what caused Mildred to be praising God so much while on the phone.

Pamela said, "I just wanted to let you all know that. I couldn't hold it. I am so happy for them. I will talk with you later."

Mildred said, "Thanks for sharing the news. Bye.

Thomas could hardly wait until Mildred got off the phone. He asked, "What was that about?"

"Well the Pirates have bought an apartment complex in Hillsboro. They want to settle down and come to ourchurch and Bible studies," Mildred said.

"Well, I'll be darned. What a blessing. Wow! It's amazing how God work some things out in life," Thomas said.

"Yes it is. They were serious about finding Jesus. I am glad that we were able to share the word with them. We never know how God is going to use us." Mildred said.

"That's why it's important for Christian to study the word and be ready to share when the opportunity arises. We never know how God is going to use us to bring someone to Him," Thomas said.

Mildred said, "When we were first captured, I was really afraid but the Holy Spirit told me that everything was going to be alright. I had no idea that it was going to turn out like this. I just had to trust God and believe that it was going to be alright. Now look what God has done."

Meanwhile the Pirates decided to convert two of the apartments into a recreation room. It would have a kitchen and two bathrooms. They want a place big enough so they could invite David, Pamela, Thomas and Mildred and other friends that they would make at the church. They started planning to have a big dinner celebration for the church. They want to show their appreciation for being accepted by the church. They had one area with three couches and had an area with tables put together like a long table. When they have dinners, people could go around the table to get what they wanted to eat. They had a couple of tables set up with chairs but they had more folding table and chairs in the closets.

This room was also used for them to get together in the evenings to play cards or dominoes and eat together. They were family so this was perfect for them. Most of them cooked real good meals.

Sometimes they would be up all night, especially on Friday nights. They made sure that on Saturday nights that they didn't stay up too late because they would be going to church on Sunday mornings. All the guys still looked at Juan Miguel Ramos as their leader. They loved Juan Miguel Ramos as their leader. They respected him very much. What he did was took all of them to the bank and opened a checking and savings account for each one of them. He explained to them that they had to start learning how to handle their money.

Juan Miguel Ramos also set time aside to show them how to handle a checking account and how to balance it. These men were very grateful that they had him and that he took time to share these things with them.

Some of the men didn't have a high school education but all of them could read and write. He was preparing them to make the transition back into society and to know how to do things that they had not learned to do.

The Pirates bought a fifteen passenger van and had the word Pirates written on it. Even though they were transitioning back into society, they would always be The Pirate family. They all were very happy that the community accepted them. Now they were getting ready to learn to live like everyone else. The right way!

Now they will be ready to think about dating once they have settled in their new place in Hillsboro. Of course they are nervous because it's been years since any of them had been on a date.
One evening when they were sitting around talking Private Donald asked Sgt. Puget, "When was the last time you dated?

Sgt. Puget said, "It's bee years ago. It wasn't serious, though."

"It will be nice to have a woman to talk to sometime," Private Donald said.

Juan Miguel Ramos said, "Just remember one thing, treat the ladies with respect and go slow so you don't get your heart broken."

Sgt. Puget said, "There's lots information on the internet about everything. I am sure we can find something about dating."

Private Pete said, "Just be yourself and everything will work out."

CHAPTER 9

The Pirates Joined Church

Now that the Pirates were settled in their living spaces, it was time to commit. When they went back to church, they were on fire for the Lord. Now they had their Bibles and had been reading the verses for Bible study. When the doors of the church were opened, for anyone to join, they all went forward.

The members were shouting and praising God like they had never done before. David, Pamela, Thomas and Mildred rushed up front and started hugging all of them. There was not a dry eye in the church.

Some of them signed up for the choir and some for the Praise and Worship Team. It was truly a happy day in Hobart and in heaven. This was a day that they all would remember. At the end of the service Pastor Higgins prayed over the Pirates. Then all the members lined up and welcomed each one of them with a hug.

Pirate Pete said, "We see what we have been missing, love and companionship with others."

Juan Miguel Ramos said, "We want to let all of you know that we are very grateful. You have opened your church and your arms to us. You will not regret it. Now that we have found Jesus, we want to live the life that He wants us to live."

David said, "We want you all to know that none of us are perfect nor do we think we are. You are still going to make mistakes but you must try not to keep making the same ones over and over. We are not here to judge anyone. We are here to love and help keep each other be accountable. We thank each of you and look forward to growing deeper in the word with you."

Mildred said, "When we were captured by you guys, we had no idea of what lay ahead but God. He is awesome! We love you all and we thank God for the privilege of knowing each of you."

Pirate Donald said, "We were lost. We didn't realize the damage that we were causing. We were just wondering Pirates on the ocean. Now that we know better, we will do better and we owe it to Jesus and to you all."

"We have been thanking God over and over for that experience because there was a lesson for us also. I learned that our faith was stronger than we thought. We learned for a fact that God said, "He will never leave nor forsake us." It's true. He was with us all the way. We also learned that you cannot judge people by the way they look. We need to pray about everything that we do and God will guide us," Thomas said.

Pamela said, "It's time for us to put this behind us and move forward. God has brought us more family and we are happy about it."

Pirate Pete said, "We have bought an apartment complete in Hillsboro so we will be able to come to church and Bible study. We are truly looking forward to this. We turned two of the apartments into a large recreation room. Give us a little time because we are planning a dinner after church one Sunday to show all of you our appreciation."

Juan Miguel Ramos said, "We all are single men. We need to know which women are single and unattached in the church. My crew and I are very respectful of women. We do not want to talk to another man's wife or woman. So if it's not out of place, maybe at the end of service next Sunday, the single women could be introduced in the church. We are not looking for someone to sleep around with. I think we all would eventually like to get married and really be settled."

Capt. Pujet said, "We respect each other and we will respect each of you. It's important for us to know this so we don't approach another mans' wife or woman."

Everyone shouted and was glad to hear that the Pirates were gentlemen. Now the married men could relax because they know that the Pirates will not be trying to get their women. Pastor Higgins thanked them for sharing this because it is very important.

They all dispersed and went their way. Before the Pirates parted from David, Pamela, Thomas and Mildred, Juan Miguel Ramos gave them their address and telephone number.

Juan said, "I guess we need cell phones now. We are going to need help on which company to use." Thomas said, "That's not a problem. There areonly two companies in the area. Their service is about the same and their price."

Juan said, "Thank you, Thomas. I guess we will be heading home. Wow! That sounds good. Home!"

Capt. Pujet said, "It feels good too."

They all laughed as they parted company. The Pirates has finally found out where they belong. They were transitioning back into society and they were happy about it.

After being in the church a couple of months, they finally got nerves to start asking the single ladies out. The ladies were just as excited as the men. Since Hobart was a small town, there were not many single young men there. Since people had started visiting and joining their church from the neighboring towns, there were plenty of single men and women.

Juan Miguel Ramos finally asked Alice out. They made a beautiful couple and did not seem to be nervous with each other. Capt. Pujet started dating Rose and most of the time the four of them doubled dated. They all got along with each other very well. There were a couple of movie theatres, four nice restaurants, bowling alley and an amusement park. There were other places to go in the surrounding towns also.

Finally the Pirates invited the church members to come to their recreation room for dinner after church for the following Sunday. Pamela, Alice, Rose and Mildred were going to do the cooking. They had fixed it up very nice. One section was tables and chairs, one area with games and the other section had couches and a television.

The church members were excited and anxious to see the Pirates establishment. And you know they were looking forwards for free food. The Pirates also had a beautiful area outside with a bar-b-que grill with tables and chairs. The Pirates were anxious to show their appreciation to the community.

These men had truly been touched by God because they all were on fire for the Lord. It was so beautiful to see them and when they sang, the people got chills.

CHAPTER 10

The Pirates Joined Church

The Pirates were truly anointed and eager to learn the word. They were faithful coming to church and Bible study. This was a whole new way for the Pirates to live. They had found a whole town of new friends, had a place to live and women to date. They did almost everything together because they were a family within themselves.

They were happy because they were shown a lot of love from the people. It's now coming up to a year that they have been in Hillsboro and Pastor Higgings has been watching them. He plans to make some of them Deacons in the church and offer a couple of them to teach a men's study class.

Pastor Higgins can see how they have grown since they joined the church. There are couples who might be getting serious. Juan Miguel Ramos and Alice were on a date.

He asked her, "What do you think about marriage?" Alice said, "If two people really love each other, theyshould get married but I believe they need to be counseled by their Pastor first."

Juan Miguel Ramos asked, "Why is that?"

Alice answered, "Well it's because the Pastor will ask certain questions and the responses will tell if the couple is stable enough for marriage."

Juan Miguel Ramos asked, "Do you think you are ready for marriage"

Alice answered, "Yes, I am ready for marriage. And then she asked, "Are You?"

Juan Miguel Ramos answered with, "I have been on the ocean a long time. I want a wife and children and I believe that I could be a good husband and father. Yes, I am ready for marriage.

Alice said, "Since you have been out of circulation so long, don't you think that you should date other women to make sure you find the right one to marry?"

Juan Miguel Ramos said, "Alice before I went on the ocean, I dated a few women but they were not what I wanted in a wife. I never met a woman that I felt like I wanted to live with for the rest of my life."

Alice asked, "Juan, what kind of woman, are you looking for?"

Juan Miguel Ramos said, "I believe that I found her in you. I know that we have only been dating for a few months but when I first saw you, I saw something special in you."

Alice is getting nervous now. Is he about to propose or what is going on? She was thinking about when she first saw him. She was immediately attracted to him. She felt his warmth and compassion when he spoke to the church to find out about the single ladies in the church. That made her to know that he would be a faithful man, someone who could be trusted.

Alice said, "It was mutual, I felt the same way about you when you spoke in the church to know which women were single. I thought that was very honorable."
By now Juan Miguel Ramos has pulled out a beautiful engagement ring.

He said, "Alice, I have grown to know you and I am very much in love with you. Will you accept this ring as a promise to marry me and be with me forever?"

Alice looked him in his big beautiful eyes and said, "Juan Miguel Ramos, I will accept your ring and promise to marry you and love you as long as I live."

They had not ever kissed in all the months that they had been dating. Now both of them were nervous. Something strange happened, Juan Miguel Ramos pulled a little away from her.

He said, "I will kiss you on our wedding day. That kiss will seal my love for you forever." He kissed her on her forehead.

Alice said, "I knew you were special and I thank you and I will never forget this moment."

Juan Miguel Ramos said, "Well my love, I should get you home at a respectful hour. It's getting late."

He hugged her when he brought her home. He was a very happy man. Alice could not believe what had happened the way it did. She thought, "I knew he was a good man and I thank God for bringing him into my life."

The following Sunday when Juan Miguel Ramos and Alice Williams' engagement was announced the church rallied around them and were happy for them.

When Alice had a chance to be with Rose, Mildred and Pamela, they could not believe how Juan Miguel Ramos had proposed to her. Most of all the fact that he did not kiss her after he proposed surprised them. They knew he was one of a kind. They were very happy for the two of them.

Alice said, "Now I see what it means to wait and let God send you a mate. When I was in my late teens, I decided not to date because of the stories my friends would tell me about their experiences. It was not what I wanted so I prayed for God to put the right man in my life and now He has done that."

Mildred said, "We are so proud of you and we are happy for you. Juan Miguel Ramos and his men stand out. They respect him and have followed his lead. They all will probably make good husbands. They are in the word and are very serious about learning how to live the way God wants them to live."

Pamela said, "It can't get any better than that. These young men are on fire for the Lord. They also are very respectful."

Rose said, "Yes they are! Sgt. Pugt. has not tried to be pushy in a sexual way. We have held hands and that's it. I like that because it shows that he respect women."

Mildred said, "We love all of the Pirates. They have shown themselves to be gentlemen. They have a good leader and that's what makes the difference."

Pamela said, "When a boy grows up without a father, it is basically hard for him to become a good man. But there are some men who grew up without a father who became good men because they had a strong mother and grandmother to guide them in knowing how to treat a woman."

Mildred said, "There are about four of them who are about to become Deacons in the church."

Alice said, "That's great. Boy they can sing."
Rose said, "Yes they can and you can see when the Holy Spirit hits them. It's like they are in their own world with God."

Mildred said, "Boy, they sure can sing those old hymns.

Rose said, "It's time for me to go. Sgt. Puget and I

are just going to be at their recreation room. You all can come and join us if you like."

Alice said, "I have some things to catch up on at home. I will see you all at Bible study."

Mildred said, "I am on my way home. Thomas is probably wondering when I going to get there."

Pamela said, "I told David that I would be coming home a little later. See you guys at Bible study."

Well the Pirates have found a place to belong and are accepted. They are happy to be settling down and living like normal people. The best part is that they not only found a whole town of friends but THEY FOUND JESUS!

BIO OF DORIS M. JONES

She was born and raised in Dallas, Texas. As a small child, she was very, very bashful and hid behind her writing. She started writing poems when she was seven or eight years old and in high school she was writing short stories.

Doris married her high school sweetheart and from that union they had five children. After divorce, she later remarried and moved to Fresno, CA and later, Clovis, CA. There she began to publish poems under her new married names Jones-Landrine.

Several of her poems were published in the Fresno Bee and different Poetry Anthologies (70 poems), which are in Public Libraries. She was voted, "Who's Who in Poetry in 2004-2005." Presently she has eight other self-published books.

Doris also has received many writing awards and her writing covers five Genres.

A NOTE FROM THE AUTHOR

God has all the power in his hands and He works in ways that we will never understand. We need to learn to lean on Him and trust His word. He said, "I will never leave you nor forsake you. I will be with you to the end of the world."

We never know how God is going to use us to bring someone to Him.

My Published Works Are:

1. I'll Wait
2. Love Has No color,
3. Joe's Most Dangerous Mission (Sequel to I'll Wait)
4. A Miracle for Sarah
5. Thoughts of Mind (Poetry)
6. How to Survive on a Little
7. Thoughts Feelings Visions Memories (Poetry)

www.ingramcontent.com/pod-product-compliance
Lightning Source LLC
Chambersburg PA
CBHW071015120626
46546CB00003B/1090